Firefighting

Illustrated by Daniel Moignot
Created by Gallimard Jeunesse
and Daniel Moignot

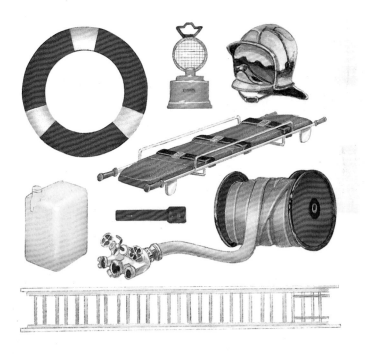

MOONLIGHT
PUBLISHING

MY FIRST DISCOVERY PAPERBACKS

Prehistoric people discovered how to make fire and how useful it is.

They also found how dangerous it is!

Fire!

Firemen are always
ready for an emergency.

This fire engine can carry
a huge amount of water.

This fire engine is
used at airports.

Firefighters all need special clothes and tools to do their work.

Fire helmet

Fireproof clothing

Torch Walkie-talkie

Key for fire hydrant

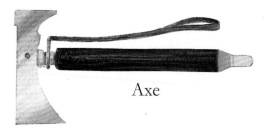
Axe

Gloves

Boots

Safety belt

Breathing apparatus

Firefighters in different countries wear different colours.

Firefighters' work is dangerous. Special clothes can save their lives.

A firefighter on standby

Protective suit against heat

Protective suit for working near explosive fuels

First aid uniform

This suit protects against chemical spills.

Diving suit

Suit for protection
against radiation

Flameproof
suit

Never play with fire!

Fire spreads very fast.
Get out. Call the
emergency services.
Stay out.

The firefighters arrive
quickly. They extend the
ladder to the top of the
house and bring everyone
down safely.

Other firefighters
put out the fire
with water from
their hoses.

This water bomber plane
fills its tanks from a lake
to put out forest fires.

The plane can drop
6 000 litres of water
on to a fire in
10 seconds.

Some firefighters work from boats or helicopters.

The ocean liner is on fire. Two fireboats are
spraying it with seawater to put the fire out.

Fires in skyscrapers are difficult to reach. These American firefighters are working from a platform below a helicopter.

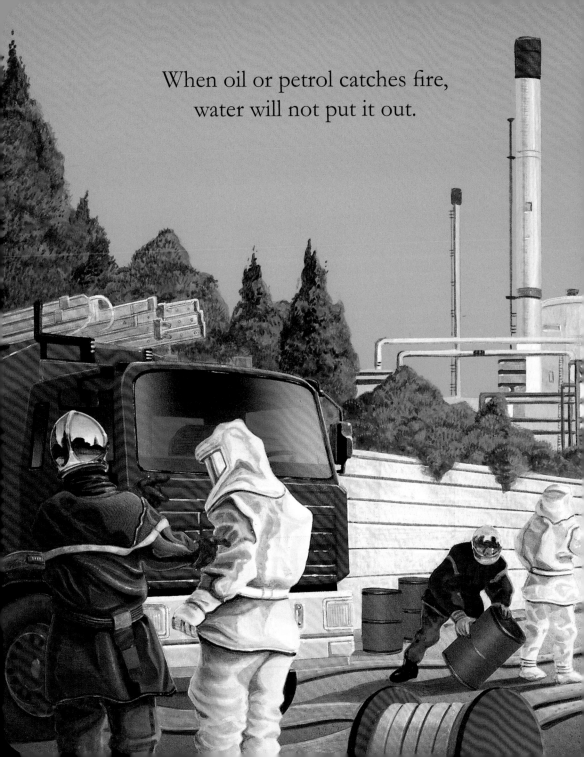

When oil or petrol catches fire,
water will not put it out.

Firefighters
use cannons
to spray foam
over the fire.

Firefighters deal with all kinds of emergencies.

They use cutting gear to free trapped passengers.

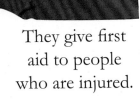

They give first aid to people who are injured.

hey rescue people who are cut off by floods.

Sometimes they use sniffer dogs to find people who are trapped under rubble.

Firefighters rescue animals too!

MY FIRST DISCOVERY PAPERBACKS

Classics

Dinosaurs
The Egg
Farm Animals
Firefighting
Flowers

Fruit
Homes
The Jungle
Planes
The Seashore

The Town
Trains
Trees
Vegetables
Water

Torchlights

Animals Underground
Arcimboldo's Portraits
Insects
Inside the Body
Life below the City

Translated by Clare Best
Editorial Advisor: Sarah Angliss
ISBN: 978-1-85103-756-8
© Éditions Gallimard Jeunesse, 2008.
English Text © Moonlight Publishing Ltd, 2022.
English audio rights ℗ Moonlight Publishing Ltd, 2022.
First published in the United Kingdom in 2022
by Moonlight Publishing Ltd,
2 Michael's Court, Hanney Road,
Southmoor, Oxfordshire, OX13 5HR,
United Kingdom
Printed in China